LEROY COLLINS LEON COUNTY PUBLIC LIBRARY

3 1260 00844 6372

W9-DBK-766

3.970.5

ON THE ROAD

TRUCKS THEN AND NOW

J 629.224 Otf
00844-6372   2-5-98   LCL
Otfinoski, Steven.

On the road : trucks
                DD

LEON COUNTY PUBLIC LIBRARY
TALLAHASSEE, FLORIDA 32301

ON THE ROAD

TRUCKS THEN AND NOW

Steve Otfinoski

BENCHMARK BOOKS

MARSHALL CAVENDISH
NEW YORK

Benchmark Books
Marshall Cavendish Corporation
99 White Plains Road
Tarrytown, New York 10591-9001

Copyright © 1998 by Steve Otfinoski
All rights reserved. No part of this book may be reproduced in any form
without written permission from the publisher.

Library of Congress Cataloging-in-Publication Data
Otfinoski, Steven.
On the road : trucks then and now / Steve Otfinoski.
    p.   cm. — (Here we go!)
Includes bibliographical references and index.
Summary: Examines the history of trucks and describes different kinds
that are used today.
ISBN 0-7614-0606-9 (lib. bdg.)
1. Trucks—History—Juvenile literature. [1. Trucks.] I. Title II. Series:
Here we go! (New York, N.Y.)
TL230.15.O84   1998   629.224—DC21   97-11562   CIP   AC

Photo research by Matthew J. Dudley

Cover photo: *FPG,* Nikolay Zurek

The photographs in this book are used by permission and through the
courtesy of: *The Image Bank:* S. Archernar, 1; Joe Azzara, 2; Kay
Chernush, 6-7, back cover; Ross M. Horowitz, 10 (bottom); Jack Ward,
20; Joe McNally, 21; Marvin E. Newman, 27; Guido Alberto Rossi, 28-29;
Anne Rippy, 32. *Corbis-Bettmann:* 7, 8, 8-9, 9 (top and bottom).
Photo Researchers, Inc.: Will McIntyre, 10 (top); Lowell Georgia, 13;
John Spragens Jr., 17 (bottom). *FPG International:* John Terence Turner,
11; Jose Luis Banus-March, 12; Ford/SB, 14; Keith Gunnar, 15; L & M
Photos, 18; Micheal Goodman, 19; John Taylor, 22 (top); R. Rathe, 22
(bottom); J. Zimmerman, 23; Chip Simons, 25. *Highway Images/Bette S.
Garber:* 16, 17 (top), 26, 30. *UPI/Corbis-Bettmann:* 24.

Printed in the United States of America

6   5   4   3   2   1

To Ben and Annie,

Keep on Trucking!

Wherever you go, you see trucks
humming down the highways.
They are carrying goods across America.
Most of what you eat, wear,
and play with came to the store by truck.
The first trucks didn't travel very far.
The one above was built in 1770 and
ran on steam.
It was used to crush walls and do other
hard work.

The first truck to run on gas (above) appeared around 1900.

The lumber truck from 1914 (center) is little more than a car with a trailer hitched to it.

By the 1920s, the first tractor trailer trucks hit the road (below right).

In the 1930s trucks became more streamlined, like this "rocket-designed" gasoline truck (above right).

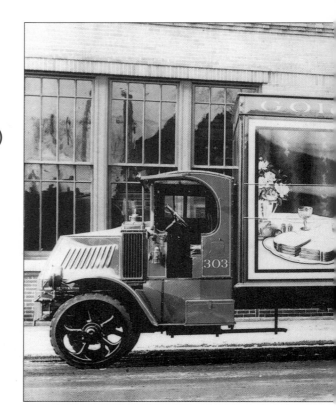

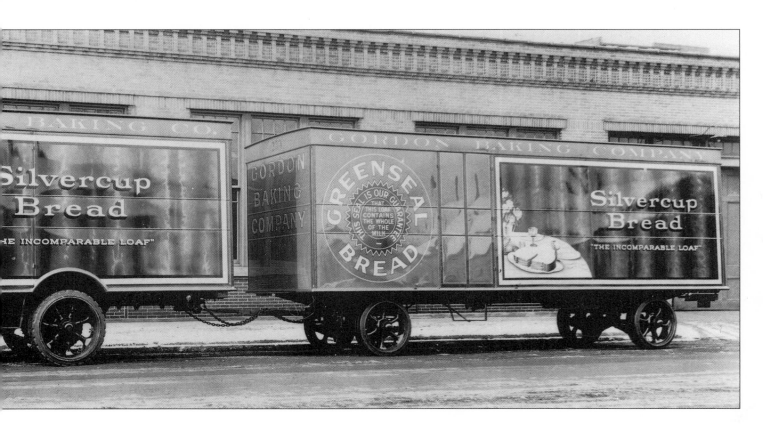

Today's modern big rigs crisscross the nation,
carrying their cargo to distant places.
They rumble over high bridges.
They roll down winding mountain roads.
They keep on trucking through sunshine, rain,
and snow.

Sometimes you can see what a truck is carrying.
The car transport truck above has a heavy load.
What do you think will happen to these logs (right)
when they get to their destination?

Sometimes you can't see what's inside a truck.
This tank truck could be carrying chemicals,
milk, or perhaps oil or gas. The liquid is pumped
through hoses to an opening on top.

Tractor trailers come in two or more sections.
The tractor includes the frame and
the cab where the driver sits.
The trailer is the part of the truck where
the cargo goes.
We don't know what's inside this triple rig,
but whatever it is, there's a lot of it!

Some truckers sleep in their trucks.

Their sleepers have all the comforts of home.

When drivers get lonely, they switch on their

CB (citizens band) radio.

They talk to other truckers in a language all their own.

"Piggy bank" is a toll booth.

"Smokey Bear" is a police officer.

"Coffeepot" is a restaurant.

Truckers look forward to stopping at roadside restaurants.

They enjoy each other's company as much as the food.

Not all trucks carry goods to market.
This colorful ready-mix concrete truck makes
concrete for construction.
The mixer spins round and round to keep the concrete
wet and ready to use.
The dump truck on the next page has a truck bed that
can be tilted up when it's time to dump the load.

Some trucks come right to your house to deliver a package, a new appliance, or a bouquet of flowers. Some trucks even deliver milk, although most people today buy their milk at the store.

Other trucks pick up.
This garbage truck is specially designed to automatically
pick up garbage cans and dump out the garbage inside.
All the driver has to do is open the lid.

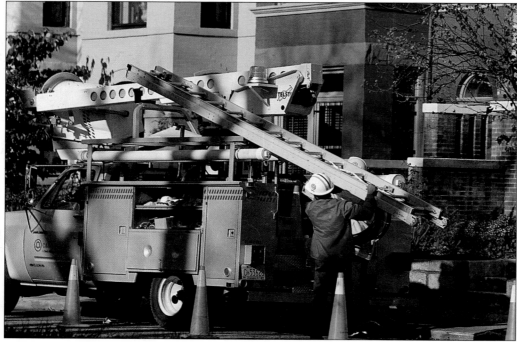

Other trucks lend a hand
when you need it.
Here's a tow truck (top left)
being towed by a tow truck!
These workers (bottom left)
are unloading a ladder from
a repair truck.
The crane that lifts the
worker up to the power lines
is called a cherry picker.
Can you think why?
Pickup trucks (right) are
handy for almost any job—
even pulling the family
trailer.

You don't mess with monster trucks!
This one (opposite page) is called the Eagle
and stands thirteen feet tall.
At special rallies, monster truckers love to ride over cars with
their enormous wheels and crush them to smithereens.
Other events at a monster truck rally include
driving through a mud bog and pulling a heavy load.
The fastest and most powerful truck is the winner.

Truckers like to race.
Trucks with high-powered engines
drag race on a straightaway.
These races are over in a blink of an eye.
Long-distance truck races in deserts and other
remote regions can last for days or weeks.
In "bobtail" races big-rig drivers unhitch
their trailers and race their tractors, or cabs.

How fast can a truck go?
This truck at a Kansas City air show
has been fitted with a jet engine.
It can really *zoom* down the track.

Whether you race them,
drive them, watch them,
or sit in the back
for the ride,
trucks are just plain fun.

INDEX

FIND OUT MORE

Broekel, Ray. *Trucks.* Chicago: Childrens Press, 1983.

Gibbons, Gail. *Trucks.* New York: HarperCollins, 1981.

Grimm, Rosemary. *Truck & Tractor Pullers.* New York: Macmillan, 1988.

Jefferis, David. *Giants of the Road: The History of Trucks.* New York: Franklin
   Watts, 1991.

Marston, Hope Irvin. *Big Rigs.* New York: Cobblehill, 1993.

STEVE OTFINOSKI has written more than sixty books for children. He also has
a theater company called *History Alive!* that performs plays for schools about
people and events from the past. Steve lives in Stratford, Connecticut, with his
wife and two children.